MW01069824

CANTLY A. ELLIOTT

Benched

Underrated Teams and Players in NBA History

DORRANCE
PUBLISHING CO
EST. 1920
PITTSBURGH, PENNSYLVANIA 15238

Dorrance Publishing Co
585 Alpha Drive
Pittsburgh, PA 15238
Visit our website at *www.dorrancebookstore.com*

ISBN: 978-1-6853-7127-2
eISBN: 978-1-6853-7971-1

Benched

Underrated Teams and Players in
NBA History

Acknowledgments

During the process of writing this book, I struggled with research, I struggled with writing and trying to piece things together. Some nights I stayed up until 12 a.m. writing knowing I had to work the next morning at 3 a.m. Sometimes I would stay up until the sun was coming through my blinds and I wouldn't sleep. Finding a healthy balance was hard at times. However, I was always able to find motivation and inspiration from a number of people, all for different reasons. I want to take a moment to thank those people for being apart of the process and always giving me a reason to believe in myself. Thank you all for being my reason and my "why" and pushing me to go the extra mile to make my dream a reality. This is for us.

God gets all of the credit. Without him I am nothing.

Craig & Roen Elliott
Ross Elliott
Rebecca & Conrad Dozier
Gloria Cantly
Bobby Cantly
Cody Cantly
Sco Elliott
Tim Elliott
Teddy Elliott
Verletta Elliott
Lavada Elliott
Keisha Cochran
Kendall Bailey
Jae'ron Boynton
Jaleel Watkins
Titan & Ebony Elliott
Rachel Orwick
The Nellessen/Orwick Family
Jaeden Bailey
The McFann Family
Jay Richardson
Clay Hall
ABC6/FOX28 Team
The Wittenberg University English Department
The Blaze Review Team

UNDERRATED
PLAYERS

Dominique Wilkins

The majority of people who watched Dominique play in the '80s and '90s certainly have a ton of respect for his game and what he did for basketball; people in my age group don't talk about him enough.

Wilkins was drafted third overall in the 1982 NBA Draft behind James Worthy and Terry Cummings. Many don't know that Wilkins was actually drafted by the Utah Jazz but due to financial reasons, Wilkins was traded to the Hawks months later. Wilkins really blossomed into a star in the 1985-1986 season when he won the NBA scoring title averaging 30.3 points per fame, made the NBA All-Star for the first time and made First Team All-NBA. In that same season, the Hawks put together a 50-32 regular season record finishing fourth in the Eastern Conference. Once the playoffs arrived, Atlanta beat the Detroit Pistons three games to one in the opening round but would lose four games to one to the Boston Celtics who went on to win the NBA title that year. Wilkins averaged 26.8 points per game in those nine playoff games.

Wilkins earned the nickname "The Human Highlight Film" for his ability to throw down monster slam dunks and leave the crowd in awe. He is widely regarded as one of the best dunkers in NBA history. I find myself on You-Tube watching his highlights: breathtaking, acrobatic moves that rock the rim in a fashion few can imitate today.

Adrian Dantley

The game of basketball has been and always will be about getting buckets. When we mention a lot of the certified "bucket getters" in NBA history, Adrian Dantley is a guy who needs to be brought up more in this discussion. Dantley was selected sixth overall in the 1976 draft by the Buffalo Braves. He had a nice season averaging 20.3 points per fame along with 7.6 rebounds per game and won the Rookie of the Year Award in 1977. After one season, the Braves traded Dantley to the Indiana Pacers where he only appeared in 23 games. Dantley was then traded to the Lakers for two seasons but really found a home and had success when he was traded to the Utah Jazz to start the 1979-1980 season.

Dantley's most impressive season with Utah had to be the 1983-1984 season. He averaged 30.6 points per game, 5.7 rebounds, and 3.9 assists while shooting 56% from the field. He also led the Jazz to the number two seed in the Western Conference behind the Los Angeles Lakers. While the season did come to a disappointing end after the Jazz lost in the second round to the number six seed Phoenix Suns four games to two, Dantley averaged 30 points per game for the fourth consecutive season.

When you look at Dantley's career as a whole, he too could easily be considered one of the most underappreciated players. It took sixteen years after his retirement to be voted into the Hall of Fame. I always wonder if he had won a major award such as MVP or played in a bigger market winning a championship or two, how would he be regarded today? He deserves more recognition for being one of the premier scorers and stars of his generation.

Bernard King

Before I even mention anything about Bernard King the player, I do want to acknowledge the scoring clinic that he put on against the Detroit Pistons in the opening round of the 1984 playoffs. The Knicks beat the Pistons four games to one with King averaging 42.6 points per and shooting over 60% from the floor.

In the final game, King played with the flu and a dislocated finger, and still managed to score 44 points to close out the series. Something else that may seem minor but is pretty incredible is that King played the last five minutes of regulation and overtime with five fouls. It may seem like a short period of time, but playing a physical, gritty team like the Detroit Pistons in an elimination game with five fouls for that long takes a substantial amount of discipline.

March 23, 1985, the New York Knicks were on the road playing the Kansas City Kings. On a fast break, King went up to block a dunk by Reggie Theus and landed awkwardly on his right leg resulting in a torn ACL, torn knee cartilage and a broken leg bone sidelining him for the rest of the 1984-1985 season as well as the 1985-1986 season. At the time, this was considered a career ending injury that almost nobody came back from.

During rehab, King was able to get back into playing shape and attempted a return to the NBA at the end of the 1987 regular season. He would only play six games and average 22.7 points per game but he was not as explosive as he was in the past and the Knicks released him at the end of the 1987 season.

The following season, King joined the Washington Bullets and was still a scoring threat for them averaging 20-plus points in three of his four seasons with the team. In the 1990-1991 season, King's scoring average was a whopping 28.4 points per game which is the second highest average of his career. King had another knee operation performed before the 1991-1992 season causing him to miss the entire season and later be waived by the Bullets in 1993. King later had a short stint with the New Jersey Nets before officially retiring from the NBA.

Just imagine if he could have moved up ONE spot in the 1977 draft over Kenny Carr, gone to the Lakers and teamed up with Kareem, Adrian Dantley, Jamaal Wilkes and Norm Nixon. That would have been one hell of a team to watch. Sadly, we will never get to witness that, but the game did get to witness a historic player in Bernard King.

Alex English

Carmelo Anthony was my first favorite NBA player growing up so I was always a Nuggets fan. My dad actually told me about Alex English when I was much older. I started to go on YouTube and watch his highlights and I remember being very impressed with how good his mid-range jump shot was. If you can't tell by now, I love watching the old school players who put up high scoring totals and averages when a lot of the game was focused on scoring inside and from the midrange back then.

As basketball fans, we associate a lot of the great scorers in NBA history with the 1980s: Michael Jordan, Larry Bird, Kareem Abdul-Jabbar and many other players. There could be an argument made that English was the best scorer in the 1980s. English averaged at least 25 points per game for eight straight seasons from 1981-1989 with a career high of 28.4 in the 1982-1983 season. He also scored 21,018 points over the course of the 80's, which was the most in the decade. When he retired, he was number seven on the NBA all-time scoring list.

One of the other conversations that would be interesting about English, is could he be in the discussion for the greatest second-round draft pick in league history or where does he fall in all-time second rounders? There have been some notable players: Manu Ginóbili, Dennis Rodman, Scottie Pippen, Nikola Jokic Draymond Green. These are all guys with titles and other accolades that I would probably put ahead of Alex English in terms of the history of the NBA. But imagine if English had a title or two to his credit or maybe an MVP. Does that change the discussion?

Alex English didn't have a flashy style of play or personality like many of the other all-time NBA greats; maybe that's why he is very rarely ever mentioned with them? Looking at the overall success and individual stats, there is no doubt that his name certainly does belong in the conversation.

Michael Cooper

When you look at Michael Cooper's stats, he is not a guy that will take your breath away. Cooper played twelve seasons all with the Los Angeles Lakers and averaged 8.9 points, 4.2 rebounds and 3.2 assists. When I study Cooper's game, he is really truly fascinating to me because I think he was truly one of the first "Three and D" guys in the NBA.

He made the NBA All-Defensive First Team five times and the All-Defensive Second Team three times. He also won Defensive Player of the Year in the 1987 season. In sports, they always say the best ability is availability and Michael Cooper was always ready to suit up. In the twelve seasons that he played, he had five straight seasons that he played in all 82 games. He also played in at least 80 games in nine of his twelve seasons.

Cooper was a part of the "Showtime" era with the Los Angeles Lakers winning five championships. The thing that was most impressive to me was Cooper was able to guard the great Larry Bird in the 1985 NBA Finals and make things difficult for him which was pivotal in the Lakers closing the Celtics out in six games.

When we talk about some of the all-time great "glue guys" on the historic NBA teams, Michael Cooper is definitely worth mentioning in the discussion. In some ways when I look at his game, he feels like an early blueprint for what good role players look like in today's NBA.

Alonzo Mourning

My first glimpse of Alonzo Mourning was when he was coming off of the bench for the Miami Heat on their championship team in 2006. He was close to the end of his career at that point, but still a relatively good rim protector averaging 2.7 blocks per game.

Mourning was drafted number two overall by the Charlotte Hornets in 1992. After three seasons in Charlotte, Mourning would later be traded to the Miami Heat where he was the star player. In his first season in Miami, Mourning averaged 23 points, 10 rebounds and 2.7 blocks per game. Miami had their fair share of struggles throughout the season but they did make the playoffs as an eight seed and played the historically great 72-win Chicago Bulls. Talk about tough luck.

The 1996-1997 season was the most successful for Mourning and the Heat. Miami won 61 regular season games which was a record at the time, and finished second in the Eastern Conference behind the Chicago Bulls. Once the playoffs rolled around, The Orlando Magic took the Heat all the way to five games but it would be Miami that would win and advance to play the New York Knicks in the conference semifinals. This was the beginning of a short-lived but very intense rivalry between the two teams. Before the 1997 season, no two teams had ever played four straight years in the playoffs and went the maximum number of games in a series before the Heat and Knicks did it. The Knicks went up 3-1 in the series but the Heat would rally a comeback and win the series in seven games advancing Miami to meet the Chicago Bulls again in the Eastern Conference Finals. The Bulls would win again in five games.

After his time in Miami, Mourning signed a four-year deal with the New Jersey Nets but retired from the NBA shortly after due to health issues. Mourning did make a return to the NBA in 2005 and rejoined the Miami Heat. As I mentioned earlier, he played a significant role coming off of the bench behind Shaquille O'Neal and even sometimes sharing the court with Shaq. Mourning provided some valuable minutes and was a key piece to the Miami Heat winning their first ever championship in the 2005- 2006 season. Mourning announced his retirement from the NBA in 2009 and was inducted into the FIBA Hall of Fame in 2019. I think when we look at the all-time great, big men who played both ends of the floor well, Mourning is among the best.

UNDERRATED
TEAMS

2012-2013 Memphis Grizzlies

In the 2012-2013 season, the Grizzlies team finished fifth in the Western conference with a 56-26 record. Imagine winning 50-plus games and finishing in the middle of your conference. Unheard of.

What made this team so good and so dangerous, mainly in the playoffs was that they had super scrappy defensive players that didn't fear anybody: Zach Randolph, Tony Allen, Rudy Gay, Mike Conley and Marc Gasol (Gasol won the 2013 NBA Defensive Player of the Year award). They held their opponents to 89.3 points per game which is the last time a team held their opponents under 90 points per game in an NBA season.

The highlight of the season came in the playoffs when the Grizzlies played the Los Angeles Clippers and found themselves down 0-2 in the series. The Grizzlies somehow found a way to win the next four straight games and advance to the next round to play my Oklahoma City Thunder.

The Thunder were a young and injured team by this point in the season and the Grizzlies would go on to win the series in five games. As we know, all good things must come to an end. The Grizzlies' exceptional playoff run came to an end when they faced a veteran San Antonio Spurs team in the conference finals and got swept in four games..

The thing that was remarkable about this season was that this team wasn't some crazy offensive juggernaut, they only posted 93.4 points per game which was 27th best in the league that season. This was a team that made a living night in and night out on the defensive end of the court and really embraced the "Grit and Grind" brand of basketball Memphis is known for.

2008-2009 Orlando Magic

This season by Orlando was VERY impressive, led by one of the most dominant, explosive young players I have ever seen, Dwight Howard. Orlando finished the season with a 59-23 record, which was a franchise best since the 1995-1996 season. They ended up earning a number three seed in the postseason. In the first round, Orlando took on a tough Philadelphia 76ers team and beat them in six games before matching up against the defending NBA champion Boston Celtics in the semifinals and beating them in seven games.

The series with Boston was a hard-fought battle and after five games, Boston was up 3-2, but the Magic were able to fight back and win game six at home and game seven in Boston. Last but not least, in the Eastern Conference Finals, the Magic ran into the number one seed Cleveland Cavaliers led by a young LeBron James looking to make his second NBA Finals appearance. The Magic would end up beating the Cavs in six games..

Looking at this playoff run as a whole, the Magic put together a very admirable and memorable run, but it would end when they played Kobe Bryant and the Lakers in the Finals and the Lakers won four games to one. I think Kobe and the Lakers were dead set on winning a championship after losing the previous season in the Finals to the Celtics.

The NBA really shifted to a three-point heavy league around the 2015-2016 season when Golden State took the league by storm. But you do have to give this Magic team credit. They actually set the record for the most threes made in a game by a team hitting 23 (which really seems like nothing now because it has been broken over twenty times since 2009). With sharpshooters like JJ Reddick, Rashard Lewis and Hedo Türkoglu, the three-point throne was established at one point in history. When you look at this team, they really were the perfect combination of the hard, physical style of play associated with the 2000s and the high volume of offense and three-point shots of the NBA today.

2014-2015 Atlanta Hawks

Almost every team in the history of basketball has a "go to" player in the clutch or a clear number one option to run their offense. This Atlanta Hawks team was unique because they didn't have a specific player, but had a variety of players they could run their offense through and every night someone different would get hot.

The Hawks got off to a rocky start in the beginning of the season posting a 9-6 record through the first month of play, but then they got hot and won 14 of their 16 games in the month of December to close out the 2014 calendar year.. In January of 2015, the Hawks posted a perfect 17-0 record and the entire starting five was named "Player of the Month" for the Eastern Conference. In February, the Hawks sent four players to the All-Star game in New York. The players were Al Horford, Jeff Teague, Kyle Korver, and Paul Millsap.

The playoffs rolled around and Atlanta was still able to play good basketball beating both the Brooklyn Nets and Washington Wizards in the first two rounds but ended up getting swept by the Cleveland Cavaliers in the Eastern Conference Finals. The Hawks became the first number one seed to get swept in a playoff series since the Detroit Pistons did in 2003. On the bright side, their 22 game improvement was the second largest by a team that made the playoffs in consecutive non-lockout years behind the 1995-1996 Chicago Bulls who won 25. Overall, this was a fun time to be a fan of the Atlanta Hawks or a fan of teams that just play good, unselfish basketball and value the whole team.

1971-1972 Milwaukee Bucks

The 1971-1972 Milwaukee Bucks had a phenomenal start to the season, posting a 17-1 record through their first 18 games of the season, and looking to dismantle the NBA just as they did the year before when they won their first NBA championship. January 9th, 1972 was an iconic night in NBA history. The Bucks matched up with the Los Angeles Lakers in a clash that will be remembered forever when the Bucks snapped the historic thirty-three-game win streak set by the Lakers. That record still stands today. At the end of the 1972 regular season, the Bucks finished with the second best record in the NBA at 63-19 behind the Los Angeles Lakers. It was as clear as day that these were the two best teams in the league and it was only a matter of time before everything came to a head.

The Bucks and Lakers would later meet in the Western Conference Finals, and this is where the "buck" stopped for Milwaukee. No pun intended, but the Lakers would win the series four games to two and advance to the NBA Finals, beating the New York Knicks to win the sixth title for the franchise.

Out of all of the teams that are mentioned in this section, the Bucks are the most impressive to me because they were an expansion team and had immediate success upon entering the league. They won a championship in 1971 and competed against elite talent in their first five years.. Not many of the expansion teams in my lifetime have accomplished such a feat.

1995-1996 Seattle Supersonics

This is another one of those teams I believe was ahead of their time similar to the Orlando Magic in 2008-2009. We all know how three-point happy the NBA is these days, but back in the 1990s, if you look at the average number of three-point shots taken back then, teams were only attempting somewhere between 7 to 16 per game. That has almost doubled in today's game. Several players on this team including Gary Payton, Hersey Hawkins and Sam Perkins were each attempting 4-4.5 three point shots per game and hitting in the mid to high thirty percent range. So they had the perimeter scoring, but the secret weapon inside was Shawn Kemp, also known as "The Reignman". I really believe he is one player from that era that was ahead of his time. His style almost gave you a "smallball" type of feel. With his size and athletic ability, I think he is one of a few players from that era who would be able to make it in today's NBA.

At the power forward/center position, Kemp did a lot of things well. His dunking ability and putting a number of defenders on a poster is what he is mainly known for, but he also had a nice midrange jump shot and could get to the bucket for a crafty finish.

The Supersonics were able to finish the regular season with a 64-18 record and secure the number one seed in the Western Conference for the third time in the franchise's history. They also had a 38-3 record at home which was second best in the league behind the Chicago Bulls. The Supersonics defeated the Sacramento Kings three games to one in the first round of the playoffs, they swept the defending champion Houston Rockets in the second round and beat the Utah Jazz in seven games in the Western Conference Finals to advance to their first Finals since 1979. The Supersonics would ultimately lose to the Bulls four games to two, but they played super hard against them and didn't make it easy. Despite never winning a championship, Gary "The Glove" Payton and Shawn Kemp are one of the most electrifying duos to ever play the game, and they had a strong, supporting cast that helped solidify this team's spot in NBA history.

1994-1995 Houston Rockets

The Rockets won the championship the year before in 1994 and they looked invincible to start the 1994-1995 starting the season 9-0 before dropping three straight. he team would later struggle after the All-Star break, finishing the season with a subpar record of 47-35, sixth place in the West, and a very tough path in the playoffs. In the first round, the Rockets were able to beat the Utah Jazz led by Karl Malone and John Stockton in five games. The second round against Charles Barkley and the Phoenix Suns would go seven games with Houston coming out on top and just like that the Rockets were back in the Conference Finals this time matching up against the San Antonio Spurs. I seriously wish I could have been around in this era of basketball because I would have loved to see the center matchup between Olajuwon and David Robinson. Looking at the stats and highlights from this series, these two were battling but Olajuwon was the more dominant of the two. He averaged 35 points, 11 rebounds, 4.5 assists and 4.2 blocks in the series giving the Rockets the edge to advance to the NBA Finals for the second year in a row.

The finals matchup featured another heavyweight battle at center between Hakeem and Shaquille O'Neal. This was the first Finals appearance by the Orlando Magic, but familiar territory for the Rockets. The more experienced Rockets would go on to sweep the Magic and boost them to another NBA championship. This postseason run by Houston is legendary for two reasons:

1. At the time, the Houston Rockets were the first team in NBA history to beat four 50-win teams to secure a championship.

2. They are still the lowest seeded team in NBA history to win an NBA championship.

2008-2009 Cleveland Cavaliers

In the 2007-2008 season, the Cleveland Cavaliers only won 45 games but they took a major leap in the 2008-2009 season, winning 66 games which is still the franchise record. A big part of the increased win total came from the Cavs improving on the defensive end of the floor. The Cavs ranked 3rd in the NBA in defensive rating, moving them up eight spots from the previous season. This was also the first season we saw LeBron start to craft his signature chase down blocks on defense. James would also go on to make the All-Defensive First Team.

Outside of the Miami Heat teams, I think this was one of the ideal rosters for LeBron being a "pass first" player. He was surrounded by an arsenal of great shooters like Daniel "Boobie" Gibson, Delonte West, Mo Williams, Wally Szczerbiak and Sasha Pavlovic who all shot high thirties to low forties from three-point range. They also had a solid rim protector and rebounder in the middle in Ben Wallace and another solid, versatile defender, rookie JJ Hickson. This team was well-balanced and had all of the pieces they needed to make a run at a championship.

This team started off full steam ahead and they were hot the entire season. It didn't matter if they were at home or on the road, they took care of business. The Cavs started 23-0 at home before losing to the Los Angeles Lakers. Two days later they lost to the Indiana Pacers on the road. This was the first time the entire season the Cavs had consecutive losses, resulting in a 39-11 record in 50 games.

Everyone thought this would be the year we would get to see LeBron and Kobe go head to head in the NBA Finals. In all honesty, I'm still bummed we never got to see it. Once the playoffs came around, the Cavs matched up against their rival Detroit Pistons in the first round and swept them in four games. The Cavs also had a clean sweep in the next round against the Atlanta Hawks. May 9th, 2009 was a significant date because the Cavs became the first team in NBA history to win seven consecutive playoff games by double-digits. On May 11th, the Cavs completed the sweep against the Hawks making it the first time in franchise history they swept consecutive playoff series. Now they had the Orlando Magic in the conference finals.

This was the Magic team that I wrote about earlier in this section so I don't think I have to go into great detail about what the Cavs were up against in this series. The two teams split the first two games in Cleveland, game two was the famous LeBron three-point buzzer beater off of the in-bounds pass. Every basketball fan remembers where they were when that happened. I still get chills watching the video. Orlando would go on to win games three and four, the Cavs won game five and Orlando would close the series out in game six ending a historic season for Cleveland basket-ball.

When you look at this team on paper, nobody would have guessed they'd be as successful as they were. It may be that acquiring some of the players at the trade deadline didn't provide the time to gel like some of the other teams in the league, but they made the most of what they had and left their mark on Cleveland Cavaliers basketball history and NBA history.

1976-1977 Portland Trailblazers

This is actually the season that the NBA and the ABA merged together to become one league. The Denver Nuggets, San Antonio Spurs, Indiana Pacers and New York Nets all joined the NBA. This is important because now you have all of the best players in one league. The expansion also changed the landscape for the postseason. The NBA playoffs expanded to six teams per conference and the division winners received a bye in the first round. So there were a lot of changes and new things happening in this season which makes it even more impressive that Portland won.

The Blazers finished the season with a 49-33 record securing a three seed for the postseason in the Western Conference. This was the first playoff appearance in franchise history for the Trailblazers. The Blazers squared off against the Chicago Bulls in the first round of the playoffs beating them two games to one, advancing to play the Denver Nuggets who were new to the NBA scene. The Nuggets had secured a number two seed in the Western Conference. David Thompson and Dan Issel were the main contributors for the Denver Nuggets and they showed that they could be a force and compete in the new NBA taking the Trailblazers to six games but ultimately losing.

The Western Conference Finals came down to the Blazers vs the number one seeded Los Angeles Lakers led by Kareem. As I mentioned before, this was the Blazers' first postseason appearance and they got matched up against a historically great franchise that had been here a ton of times. That didn't matter to the Trailblazers; they actually swept the Lakers in four games to advance to the NBA Finals to face off against the Philadelphia 76ers.

The 76ers were led by Julius "Dr. J" Erving who had taken the New York Nets to the ABA title in the previous season. Something cool about this finals matchup is that five of the ten starting players between both teams came from the ABA: Dr. J, Caldwell Jones, George McGinnis, Dave Twardzik and Maurice Lucas. So this goes to show that the ABA guys were no joke and actually came to the NBA to compete.

One of the other unique things about this season is the Trailblazers became the second team in NBA history to lose the first two games of the Finals and then win the next four. That's right, the Trailblazers dropped the first two games of the series but then ripped off four straight wins giving the Trailblazers their first NBA title.

The Blazers' path to a championship was very unique compared to other teams throughout league history. This was their first season with a winning record, and the first time being in the postseason, with new players and teams from the ABA. Finally, all of the best players were now in one league, capping off their season with a historic Finals comeback. Not many teams can say they had a run like the 1976-1977 Trailblazers.

2004-2005 Detroit Pistons

The Detroit Pistons were looking to defend their title as reigning NBA champions after stunning the basketball world by beating the Los Angeles Lakers in the Finals in the previous season. The Pistons had a dominant season winning 54 games and getting the number two seed in the playoffs behind the Miami Heat, who had just acquired Shaq from the Lakers in the off-season. Once the playoffs rolled around, the Pistons beat the Philadelphia 76ers in the first round in five games and then beat the Indiana Pacers in the second round in six games. The Pistons found themselves in the conference finals for the third year in a row, this time playing the Miami Heat. The Pistons were down in the series 3-2 but destroyed the Heat in game six to tie the series and eventually beat them in game seven, and the Pistons were headed back to the NBA Finals.

This time around the Pistons played the San Antonio Spurs, a team who was well coached and familiar with the big stage but the Pistons didn't budge or roll over for the Spurs. This was the first time in eleven years that the NBA Finals had gone to a game seven. The Pistons had momentum after winning game six, but the Spurs had home court advantage where they would win their third championship in franchise history.

The Pistons had a couple of more successful seasons after their Finals victory and they were always a force to match up with in the regular season and postseason. They never really had a superstar player, but the combination of Chauncey Billups, Richard Hamilton, Tayshaun Prince, Rasheed Wallace and Ben Wallace played well as a cohesive unit night in and night out.

Over the years, debates in sports, especially basketball, have always been fun for me because it offers so many different perspectives from so many different people. A few of my favorite debate topics are: LeBron or Michael Jordan, the Showtime Lakers or the 2017 Golden State Warriors? Best Point Guard of all-time Magic Johnson or Stephen Curry?

Those are all household names, but the reality is there are so many individuals and teams who have helped shape the game of basketball into what it is today. Even the underrated ones.